THE HOUSE OF SHADOWS AND LIGHT

A STORY WITH PICTURES

KEN TATE

PHOTOS BY KEN TATE

Copyright © 2019 by Ken Tate

All rights reserved. This book or any portion thereof may not be reproduced or used in any manner whatsoever without the express written permission of the publisher except for the use of brief quotations in a book review.

ISBN 978-1-951465-63-6 hardcover

Pearl Press, LLC
PO Box 2036
Del Ray Beach, Florida
33483

THE ARCHITECT'S FOREWORD

This House calls to me. I designed her and I photographed her. I love her and I know she has soul and animation. She wants me to know that she is alive.

Every house that has soul speaks to and nurtures its occupants. They miss her when they leave her, and they are comforted by her when they return. Such houses have the spirit of the world in them — the *anima mundi*. If they are abandoned, they die a little bit each day.

They are like us. We make them and so they share our qualities — they are anthropomorphic that way. This House spoke to me. She gave me her voice for this story. It is not my voice; I am only her channel. I was possessed by her before she was even here. Or has she always been here?

THE HOUSE is alive. She has feelings. She hears the wind and the laughing children. She sees the light and shadows on her walls. She feels the rain on her roof. These things give the House joy.

THE HOUSE could not remember her first day of awareness, only an undeniable impression of being alive. Perhaps it was the first day the occupants moved into her. That day the House awoke and was filled with energy and joy. The House's heart started to open and expand to the occupants. The House was made of materials but sensed that she had a spirit as well. She desired to be of service and to know more about herself and the outside world. She could feel herself expanding each time she comforted or protected her occupants. Her materials had more energy, more spirit in them. The House knew this about herself.

THE HOUSE listens to the people who occupy her — their happiness and sorrow, their love for each other and for her. The House cherishes their love and wants to protect them. She gives them comfort and sanctuary from the world.

THE HOUSE knows morning arrives when everyone, especially children, begin to scurry around on her wood and stone floors. Their feet are like tiny massages that delight the House.

THE HOUSE misses the people when they are gone. There is sorrow in the void they leave. When they return, the House is happy and filled with purpose. The House is a Home when they are with her.

THE HOUSE has the spirit of the world in her parts and her Being. She feels connected to the natural world because she was brought forth from it. Her materials once lived there. All of these parts are now happy to be of use to the House and her occupants. They feel deeply the spirit of the people.

THE HOUSE watches the people grow and become older and wiser. She knows how hard the world can be and has compassion for them. If there is sorrow in her people, the House knows and feels that. The House is one with the hopes and dreams of her occupants.

THE HOUSE loves her outer self and her beautiful shapes and forms. It delights her to stand on the Avenue among her stately neighbors. She likes the trees and gardens that were so carefully planted in her yard and near her walls. The plantings give comfort to the House. One day the gardeners planted blooming vines on some of her walls. This made her so happy and grateful. She likes being adored and adorned. Now more people would admire the House with the lovely flowers on her walls.

THE HOUSE had many names. People call her The Villa, The Stone Lady, The Corner House and The Tower House. But the names she gives herself are The House of Shadows and Light, The House of Many Memories and The Poet's House.

There is a Poet in the House. She writes and recites poems all day long and the House absorbs them all. The House is nurtured by the poems and by their author's love of words and rhymes. The House knows in her Being that she had been brought forth by a Poet of materials and form, and that there is kinship among these things.

THE HOUSE has many walls covered with works of art. She talks to them through these walls. Sharing beauty and wisdom, they are kindred spirits who become all the greater for their friendship. The art brings more life to her walls and nurtures her. Poetry, art, gardens, and mostly, her people sustain the House. These are her lifeblood. They fill her with abundant consciousness.

THE HOUSE enjoys the way the occupants fill her with special and beautiful things — furnishings for her rooms and fabrics for her windows. The House feels the beauty of these things and they give her deeper and richer understanding of the people's needs and longings. The House feels more enriched and blessed each time they give her attention and care, adjusting her adornments with the passage of time. She revels in the ways her occupants enrich her walls and floors.

THE HOUSE cherishes memories, deep within her walls, of Another who visited often, whispering to her Essence and touching her surfaces. She senses that this must be her Creator. He knows more about the House than anyone else — every surface, space and rhythm — as though they were one. He is a magician who reminds her of the Poet who lives there. Both speak the language of beauty. When her Creator talks, the occupants listen and rejoice in his observations about the House and how she has grown even more beautiful over time. This is important to her and to her people.

THE HOUSE has many different parts given by her creator — porticos, galleries, balconies, pergolas, a loggia. Her most prized part is the Tower that ascends to the sky, allowing her to see above the rooftops. Inside the tower's room, windows on all sides invite light and shadows to dance on the walls throughout the day. The House knows where the sun is at any point. And at night the stars and moon are ever present. It delights the house to be connected to the cosmos. She shines in the starlight.

THE HOUSE, from time to time, takes inventory of herself. Her roof, her walls, columns, arches, vaults, beams, paneled ceilings, doors, windows, cabinets, plaster moldings, patterned floors — there are so many things to review. It pleases the House to look deeply into herself and marvel at her beauty and the miracle of her existence. She is aware that she has a soul.

One day, a storm came, a fierce storm.

THE HOUSE made herself strong and protected her occupants with all of her will and determination. The occupants were afraid but were calm and quiet. All the noises were on the outside — they were fierce and violent. Things were thrown at the House by the angry wind. The House was happy to protect the living ones — they gave her joy and the House would be sad if something happened to any of them. The Poet said — *the storm will pass, as do all things. The sun will rise again and we shall all be happy once more. This House is so fine and brave — it is protecting us and we owe it our lives. Let us always be grateful for its strength, beauty and comfort. Sometimes I think it is alive and that it knows our deepest needs and desires.*

THE HOUSE was tired but satisfied that her occupants were all safe and healthy after the storm. There were gardeners cleaning up the yard and workers on the roof and on ladders making repairs. The House loved her occupants for their ability to care for the House and her injuries. No bond could be stronger.

Once there was a large party at night and all the lights were on in the House.

THE HOUSE glowed with an inner fire. So many people were happy and having fun. There was noise and dancing and revelry and the House felt more alive than ever before. Her walls and floors tingled with a pleasure she had never known. The people leaned on her walls and glided on her floors and stairs, giving her a profound sense of belonging. Everything that occurred within her walls and on her lawns deepened her sense of being a part of the world. She became a House of Belonging.

THE HOUSE, at Peace, slept a deep sleep — perhaps to dream — beneath the light of a Full Moon.

ABOUT THE AUTHOR

Born in Columbus, Mississippi, acclaimed architect **KEN TATE** finds truth, beauty and soul in architecture. Over his 35-year career, Ken has designed over 70 houses in 16 states and the Caribbean and been published extensively in magazines and books. The first four monographs of his architectural work were published by Images Publishing Company. In 2019, he was awarded a Mizner Award from the Florida Chapter of the ICAA for a single residence over 10,000 square feet. Dividing his time between New Orleans and Palm Beach where his two offices are located, he enjoys the beach, looking at houses, painting and writing.

AMAZON
https://amzn.to/2G0YRaf

FACEBOOK
www.facebook.com/kentatedesign

WEBSITE
www.thektfoundation.com

PINTEREST
https://www.pinterest.com/kentate/

OTHER BOOKS BY AUTHOR
New Classicists: Selected Houses of Ken Tate, Volume 1
New Classicists: Selected Houses of Ken Tate, Volume 2
The Classic House: Windy Hill
A Classical Journey: The Houses of Ken Tate
The Alchemy of Architecture: Memories and Insights from Ken Tate
The Architect by Ken and Duke Tate, a work of fiction
Ken Tate in B & W: Architecture from a Cinematic Perspective
Architecture in Search of a Soul by Ken Tate

www.ingramcontent.com/pod-product-compliance
Lightning Source LLC
Chambersburg PA
CBHW060505240426
43661CB00007B/930